THE SECRET WORLD OF EASTER EGGS

HIDDEN FEATURES OF THE WEBSITES YOU KNOW AND LOVE

JAMES DORRIAN

DISCLAIMER

All information in this book was correct at the time of publication. However, the author apologises in the event of any out of date links or features mentioned.

CONTENTS

1   Introduction   1

2   YouTube   3

3   Google   6

4   Facebook   10

5   Wikipedia   12

6   Konami Code Easter Eggs   13

7   Some of the Best Easter Eggs from Various Sites   16

8   Mozilla Firefox   20

9   A Few Software Easter Eggs Worth Mentioning   22

1 INTRODUCTION

Having always been a bid of an avid 'treasure hunter', the world of Easter eggs has always been something of an interest of mine. If you're reading this, you probably already know what an Easter egg is. No, I'm not talking about those chocolate things you're given at Easter that you can't help but consume until the point of sickness (or is that just me?). An Easter egg, in computing terms, is a piece of hidden programming; something a developer will code into a program or website which is not immediately obvious, but is inevitably discovered by nerds like me who enjoy looking for that sort of thing.

The internet is full of such examples. Some sites, such as YouTube and Google love to indulge in providing often useless yet pleasing surprises for its users. There is always something almost childishly exciting about finding something 'hidden' on a website, as if you've stumbled across some buried treasure.

From YouTube's hidden game of Snake to Facebook's piratespeak, this book delves into the secret world of the internet to bring you some of the best of these simple delights.

Where text needs entering, I have often included this text within quotation marks ("). However, it should be noted that the quotation marks are not actually part of the string that needs to be typed out.

2 YOUTUBE

The Harlem Shake!

Type "Do the Harlem Shake" into the search bar. Watch what happens and enjoy!

Snake

Go to any video, and full screen it. Then press the left and up arrow buttons simultaneously. A giant game of Snake should appear over the top of the video that you can play while the video continues in the background.

The Wadsworth Constant

Once upon a time, a user on Reddit named Wadsworth posted that for EVERY video on YouTube, the first 30% can be skipped as it contains no useful information. This quickly became an internet meme, known as The Wadsworth Constant. In homage to this, if you add "&wadsworth=1" to the end of any YouTube video it will begin playing from 30% through.

Use the Force

Type "Use the force Luke" into the search bar. Then wait a few seconds, and watch as the page steadily rearranges itself.

Beam Me Up Scotty!

Try typing "Beam me up Scotty" into the search bar. Watch as the search results are slowly 'beamed' in!

Missile Command Game

Go to any video. Click anywhere on the page away from the video that isn't a link or a text box, then type "1980". The video should move down to make way for a Missile Command game, which you can then play.

POW Button Feature

Go to the video located at:

https://www.youtube.com/watch?v=-m_S-IDs3Wg

Now try adding "&pow=1&nohtml5=1" to the end of the URL in the address bar. There should now be an extra button at the bottom of the video player which says 'POW'. Try clicking this while the video is playing to see what happens!

Nerd Stats

Right click on any video and there should be an option that says "Stats for nerds". Click on this to see stats appear that only the truest of nerds will understand!

Doge Meme

Type "Doge meme" into the search bar. Watch as the page's fonts turn to the classic Comic Sans font.

Completely Pointless!

View YouTube's Robots.txt file by visiting www.youtube.com/robots.txt

The second and third lines read:

```
# Created in the distant future (the year
2000) after
# the robotic uprising of the mid 90's
which wiped out all humans.
```

3 GOOGLE

Six Degrees of Kevin Bacon

Surprisingly few people know this one! Type in any actor's name, followed by the words "bacon number". Google will tell you the actor's value in relation to the Six Degrees of Kevin Bacon game, including which films connect them.

Pacman

Typing "Google Pacman" into the search bar will bring up Google's version of the classic game for you to play.

The Game of Life

Search for "Conway's game of life", and then watch the right hand side of the page as Google re-enacts John Conway's 1970s cellular automation.

Recursion

Searching for the word "Recursion" will cause Google to recursively ask, "Did you mean *Recursion*".

Zerg Rush

Type "Zerg rush" into Google and then wait a few seconds. Gradually, O's will appear from the edges of the screen and begin to destroy everything on the page. You can counteract this by clicking on the O's repeatedly to destroy them.

Blink HTML

Searching for "Blink HTML" in Google will cause the words Blink and HTML in the search results to flash continuously.

Extra Space

Try searching for the word "Kerning". Every time this word appears in the search results it will have increased spacing between the letters. Then try searching for the word "Keming" This will have the opposite effect, with decreased spacing between letters.

Hidden Breakout Game

Type "Atari Breakout" into Google, then click Images and wait a couple of seconds. A game of Breakout should appear for you to play!

Tilt

Type "Tilt" into Google. Watch as the page does exactly that! (Typing "Askew" also has the same effect).

Google's Barrel Roll

Type "Do a barrel roll" into Google. See if you can get what will happen to the contents of the page! (Typing "z or r twice" also does the same thing).

Bletchley Park

Type "Bletchley Park" into Google, and on the right hand side you will see Google 'decipher' a code into the words Bletchley Park. This is in tribute to the UK's Code and Cypher school which was previously in this location.

Old Google

Type in "Google in 1998" and click Search. Google will revert to its old appearance.

Festivus

Search for "Festivus". Watch as a Festivus pole appears to the left of the search results.

Anagram

Search for the word "Anagram". Google will ask is you meant "Nag A Ram", which is an anagram of the word anagram.

Google Maps TARDIS

This one may be a bit of a pain to copy if you're reading this in paperback format, but if you're on the Kindle it should appear as a link. Go to:

https://www.google.com/maps/@51.492159,-0.192966,3a,75y,296.8h,70.44t/data=!3m5!1e1!3m3!1sH5F WWz1tdn4AAAQIt7zt5A!2e0!3e2?hl=en

You should see something that resembles the TARDIS from Doctor Who on the left hand side. Double click on this for a closer look inside!

Google Earth's Hidden Flight Sim

Open Google Earth and then press Ctrl, Alt and A simultaneously. You can now fly your F-16 plane around the world!

4 FACEBOOK

Turn Facebook Into a Pirate

This is always an amusing thing to try. On Facebook, go to your settings. Under Language, from the drop down box select "English (Pirate)". Buttons and links will now be written in pirate language!

Turn Text Upside Down

If you manage to gain access to your friend's Facebook account when they accidentally leave themselves logged in, but don't wish to do anything too harsh, this is always a good option. Go to settings, and again click to edit the language, but this time select "English (Upside Down)". Watch the bemused expression on your friend's face next time you see them log into their Facebook account!

Have Fun With Facebook Images

Next time you're chatting on Facebook, if you refer to a

friend, instead of writing their name you can have it appear as their profile pic. To do this, write their username inside double square brackets – you can find their username by going to their profile page and looking at the part of the URL after 'facebook.com/'. So if their username is 'davidbarnes', for example, you would type "[[davidbarnes]]" and it will replace the text with their profile pic. Cool, eh?

5 WIKIPEDIA

Intentional Blank Page

There is no obvious reason for this Easter Egg. If you go to "en.wikipedia.org/wiki/Special:BlankPage", a page will appear entitled 'Blank page'. The only text on this page says, 'This page is intentionally left blank.'

Hidden Easter Eggs Image

Search Wikipedia for "Easter egg (media)". Then, on the image that appears on that page, click on the hedgehog. A picture will appear of some Easter eggs.

6 KONAMI CODE EASTER EGGS

The Konami code will be familiar to many fans of Konami games from the 80s and 90s. Entering this code often unlocked hidden features within their games. This code is now used on many websites to access Easter eggs.

The code is: up, up, down, down, left, right, left, right, B and then A. Use this code on the following websites for some hidden treats.

Soundclick.com

Go to www.soundclick.com and without pressing anything else first, enter the Konami code. A huge piece of bacon should appear on the screen for you to 'eat' with your mouse.

Digg.com

Go to Digg.com and enter the Konami code. This will enable you to access a delightful musical treat!

Zeno.name

Go to zeno.name and enter the Konami code for a special message.

Kahale.net

Enter the code to view a message that makes more sense than anything else on this site.

Buzzfeed.com

Probably one of my favourite Konami Easter eggs. Go to buzzfeed.com and enter the code to see a delightful variety of sloths.

Shirtoid.com

Entering the Konami code should cause lots of dancing aliens to appear in the background. At least, that's what I think they are...

Cornify.com

Enter the code on the home page, and then watch a pony appear. Keep clicking your mouse button for a whole world of ponies!

Geekandhype.com

Go to www.geekandhype.com and enter the code for a true retro gaming experience.

Lockfale.com

While on lockfale.com, enter the Konami code for some music horse entertainment.

7 SOME OF THE BEST EASTER EGGS FROM VARIOUS WEBSITES

Hema.nl Animation – Must See!

Hema.nl is a Dutch e-commerce website that you're probably not likely to have too much call to visit. Yet it contains an Easter egg that is surely one of the best on the internet. Simply go to http://producten.hema.nl and then hover your mouse over then blue cup on the top right. Then sit back and enjoy!

Hidden Pterodactyl at Theoatmeal.com

Go to www.theoatmeal.com and then right click, and then View Source. In the source code you will see a huge image of a pterodactyl with a rather menacing message!

Skybet.com

If you're bored enough with your job that you end up

placing bets instead of working, Skybet are only too happy to help. Just above the Facebook share button on the right hand side is another button which, when clicked, will bring up a page which resembles an exceptionally dull looking spreadsheet. Perfect for when the boss appears unexpectedly!

Thcnet.net Zork 404

Go the www.thcnet.net and try to go to a page that doesn't exist (for example, www.thcnet.net/nonexistantpage). Instead of displaying a 404 error, you will be presented with the classic text-based game of Zork.

Wordpress Terms Treat

Let's face it, nobody reads through the lengthy terms and conditions that websites always expect you to agree to. Wordpress, however, have a hidden treat in theirs for anybody who's actually taken the time. Head over to http://en.wordpress.com/tos and check out term number 16…

Amazon Letter

Go to Amazon.com and then go to 'Full Store Directory', which you'll find at the bottom of the 'Shop by Department' menu. Scroll right to the bottom of the screen. At the very bottom, underneath they copyright notice, there is a hidden link – click this to find a thank you letter from CEO Jeff Bezos, to David Risher, a former Vice President who helped turn the site into the superpower it is today.

IMDB Spinal Tap In-Joke

On imdb.com, search for the film "This is Spinal Tap". When you've found it and you're on the page, look at the rating and you'll notice it's out of 11, instead of the usual 10. If you've seen the film you'll understand this reference...

Delightful Fart Sounds on Vimeo.com

On vimeo, enter the word "fart" into the search box and press enter. Now scroll up and down, and listen to some delightful examples of your search term.

Kickstarter's 'Secret' Newsletter

Go to Kickstarter.com and scroll right to the bottom of the page. Near the bottom, just above the footer, there is a small pair of scissors. Keep clicking the scissors – they will move along the page as you do. After you have clicked them three times, you will receive an invitation to be added to their 'secret' newsletter.

Wistia's Dancing Team

A very creative Easter Egg can be found at:

http://wistia.com/about/yearbook

Go to that URL and then type in the word "dance" on your computer keyboard. Enjoy the results!

Black Acre Brewing's Special Surprise

Head over to http://blackacrebrewing.com. A message will appear asking you to confirm whether you are 21. Click on 'I am under 21' for a special surprise – whatever you're expecting, it's not this!

8 MOZILLA FIREFOX

Quotes from the Book of Mozilla

Typing "about:mozilla" into the address bar will provide you with a page containing a quote from the "Book of Mozilla". Although there is no real book of Mozilla, these are styled as a kind of biblical quote, and differ between versions of Firefox. The quotes generally reference the fall of Internet Explorer as the predominant browser due to Firefox's rise over the years. Firefox is referred to as 'The Beast', while Internet Explorer is called 'Mammon'.

Robots

Type "about:robots" into the address bar and press enter. A humorous educational page about robots will appear.

Firefox Within Firefox

Type "chrome://browser/content/browser.xul" into the address bar. This will cause another Firefox window to appear within the current one. You can repeat this as many times as you like, but be aware that this is a completely useless waste of your time!

9 A FEW SOFTWARE EASTER EGGS WORTH MENTIONING

Amazon Kindle

These Easter Eggs can be found on older versions of the Kindle (specifically versions with the full keyboard).

Minesweeper

From the Home screen, press Alt, Shift and M simultaneously. A workable version of Minesweeper will appear on screen.

GoMoku

Again, from the Home screen, press Alt, Shift and M simultaneously to begin Minesweeper. However, once Minesweeper has appeared, instead of starting the game, press G. A game of GoMoku will now appear instead.

Windows 7

God Mode

I wanted to include this because it is actually a really useful feature to know. Create a new folder anywhere, and name it:

GodMode.{ED7BA470-8E54-465E-825C-99712043E01C}.

Make sure you include the full stop / period at the end. The folder will then automatically rename itself to GodMode and will contain 270 items, enabling to you configure virtually everything you could ever wish for within Windows.

Windows XP

Windows Speech Trick

Under Control Panel, open up the 'Speech' options. Select 'Microsoft Sam' as the voice, and then where it says preview, enter "Crotch" and click on Preview Voice. The voice will then say 'Crow's nest', instead of 'crotch'. Strange, but true.

Pinball Cheat

Open up the built in Pinball game (under the Start menu, All programs, Games, Pinball) and wait until the ball appears. Then type "hidden test". You should now be able to control the ball with your mouse by holding down the left button, enabling you to build up a high score easily.

Solitaire Cheat

This is an easy way to build up a lot of points in Solitaire. Start a game under the Timed and Standard options, and then keep playing for at least thirty seconds. Then press Alt, Shift and 2 simultaneously – this will end the game but will add a bonus to your score and play a celebration as if you have won. You can keep doing this as many times as you like to build up a high score.

ABOUT THE AUTHOR

James Dorrian is an avid gamer, internet enthusiast and
web designer. He currently lives in North Yorkshire,
England, with his wife and son.